GUITAR Worship CHORDS

Photos & Diagrams for 144 Chords

Contents

ISBN 978-1-61774-013-8

HAL•LEONARD®
CORPORATION

7777 W. BLUEMOUND RD. P.O. BOX 13819 MILWAUKEE, WI 53213

In Australia Contact:
Hal Leonard Australia Pty. Ltd.
4 Lentara Court
Cheltenham, Victoria, 3192 Australia
Email: ausadmin@halleonard.com.au

Copyright © 2010 by HAL LEONARD CORPORATION
International Copyright Secured   All Rights Reserved

No part of this publication may be reproduced in any form or by any means without the prior written permission of the Publisher.

Visit Hal Leonard Online at
www.halleonard.com

How to Use This Book

Each chord is identified by its symbol: **Csus4**

By its full name: **C suspended fourth**

And by its spelling:

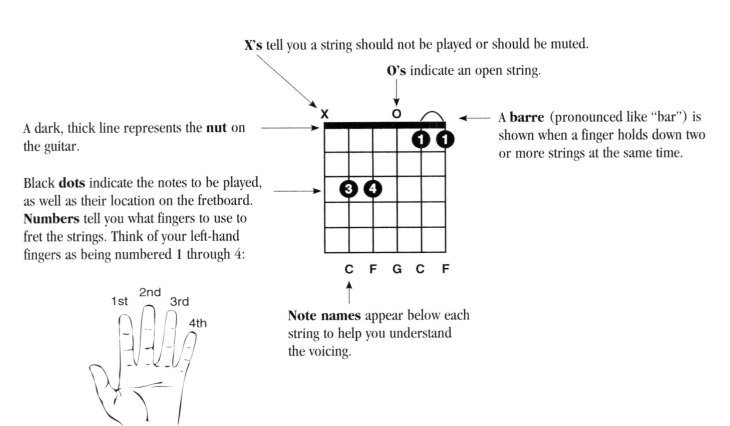

Then, you are given one common voicing for each chord, presented with a chord grid and a photo. In a chord grid, the six vertical lines represent the six strings on the guitar, from low E to high E, moving left to right. The horizontal lines represent the frets.

X's tell you a string should not be played or should be muted.

O's indicate an open string.

A **barre** (pronounced like "bar") is shown when a finger holds down two or more strings at the same time.

A dark, thick line represents the **nut** on the guitar.

Black **dots** indicate the notes to be played, as well as their location on the fretboard. **Numbers** tell you what fingers to use to fret the strings. Think of your left-hand fingers as being numbered 1 through 4:

Note names appear below each string to help you understand the voicing.

Chords above the fifth fret use a **fret number** (e.g., "5 fr") to the right of the chord grid. This tells you to move your hand up to that fret to position your fingers.

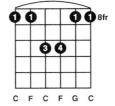

☞ One of the goals of this book is to provide "playable" chord fingerings. The fingerings in this book were chosen for their ease of play and transition between other chords in a progression. If you feel more comfortable with an alternate fingering, feel free to use it. Remember, these fingerings are only recommended. There is no single right way to play these chords.

Using a Capo

A capo is a device that clamps onto the neck of the guitar, barring across the strings at whichever fret you choose. In essence, it becomes a moveable nut, allowing you to raise the pitches of all six open strings evenly without having to retune the guitar. There are a few different types of capos available, but the "quick change" type is the most popular.

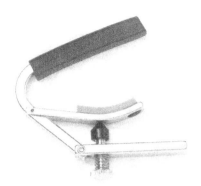

Shubb "Original" Capo

Kyser "Quick Change" Capo

When playing worship songs (or any songs for that matter), using a capo can make life much easier. For example, you can:

- **Avoid barre chords:** This is a big one, because let's face it—barre chords are simply no fun. With a capo, you can reduce the number of barre chords needed to play a song, or even eliminate them altogether!

- **Adjust the key of a song to be more "singer-friendly":** Let's say you've learned the chords for a song, but the melody is hard to sing in that key. No problem! Just use a capo to instantly transpose the song to a more suitable key, without having to learn different chords.

HOW DOES IT WORK?

Starting from the nut, each fret progressively raises the pitch of an open string by one half step. By using the capo as a moveable nut, you can raise the pitch of all six strings at once. The following example shows a D chord played in open position, and then the same D chord played with a capo on the 2nd fret acting as the nut. The capo raises the chord two half steps to sound like an E chord.

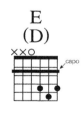

As shown in the second photo, the capo should be placed close to the fret, but not directly on top of it. (You may need to adjust the position slightly to avoid buzzing strings.)

Remember: Using a capo changes the pitch of the chords you play. This is fine if you're the only one playing. If other instruments are involved, however, those players will need to read different chords to match your sound. For example, if you're playing a song in the key of G with a capo on the 2nd fret, a keyboardist and bassist will need to play in the key of A (two half steps higher).

C (Cmaj)
C major

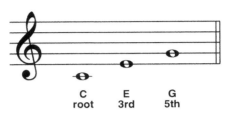

C — root
E — 3rd
G — 5th

 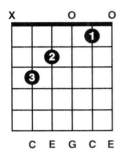

C E G C E

Cm (Cmin, C-)
C minor

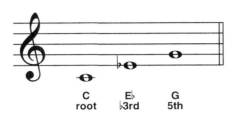

C — root
E♭ — ♭3rd
G — 5th

 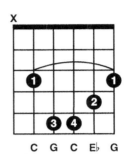

C G C E♭ G

C7 (Cdom7)
C dominant seventh

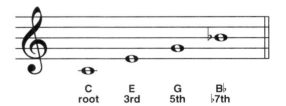

C — root
E — 3rd
G — 5th
B♭ — ♭7th

 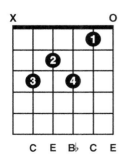

C E B♭ C E

Cm7 (Cmin7, C-7)
C minor seventh

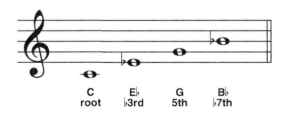

C — root
E♭ — ♭3rd
G — 5th
B♭ — ♭7th

 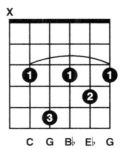

C G B♭ E♭ G

Cadd9
C added ninth

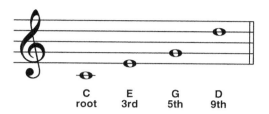

C — root
E — 3rd
G — 5th
D — 9th

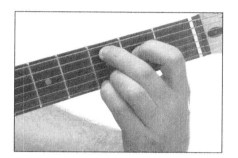 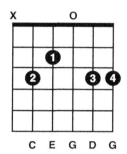

C E G D G

Csus2 (C5add2)
C suspended second

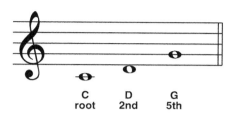

C — root
D — 2nd
G — 5th

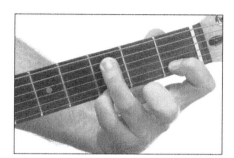 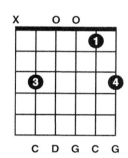

C D G C G

Csus4 (Csus)
C suspended fourth

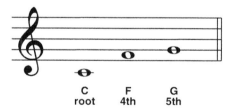

C — root
F — 4th
G — 5th

 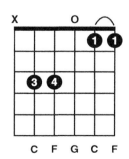

C F G C F

C7sus4 (C7sus)
C dominant seventh, suspended fourth

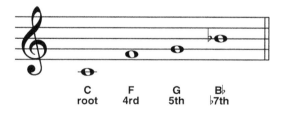

C — root
F — 4rd
G — 5th
B♭ — ♭7th

 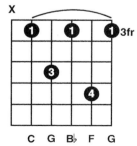

3fr

C G B♭ F G

C5 (C no 3rd)
C fifth (power chord)

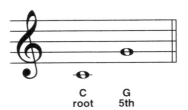

C	G
root	5th

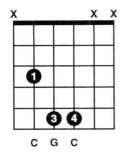

C G C

C+ (Caug, C(♯5))
C augmented

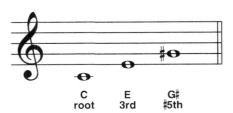

C	E	G♯
root	3rd	♯5th

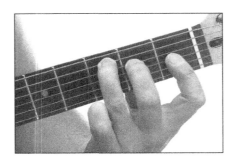

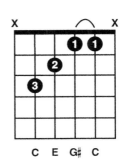

C E G♯ C

Cmaj7 (CM7)
C major seventh

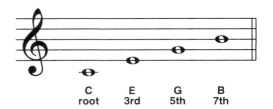

C	E	G	B
root	3rd	5th	7th

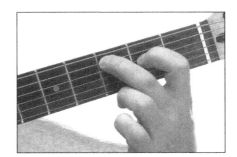

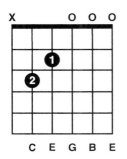

C E G B E

C°7 (Cdim7)
C diminished seventh

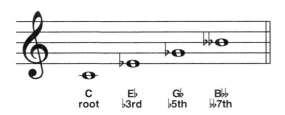

C	E♭	G♭	B♭♭
root	♭3rd	♭5th	♭♭7th

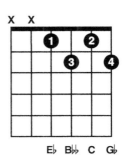

E♭ B♭♭ C G♭

C# (C#maj)
C-sharp major

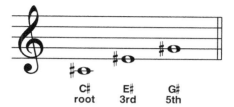

C#
root

E#
3rd

G#
5th

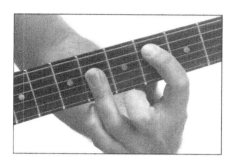

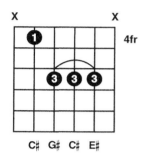

4fr

C# G# C# E#

C#m (C#m, C#-)
C-sharp minor

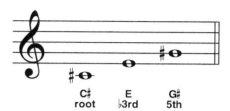

C#
root

E
♭3rd

G#
5th

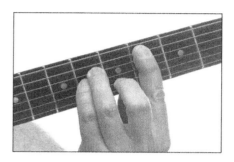

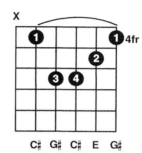

4fr

C# G# C# E G#

C#7 (C#dom7)
C-sharp dominant seventh

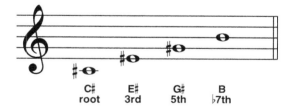

C#
root

E#
3rd

G#
5th

B
♭7th

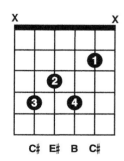

C# E# B C#

C#m7 (C#min7, C#-7)
C-sharp minor seventh

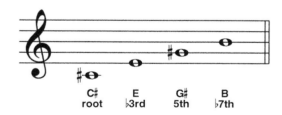

C#
root

E
♭3rd

G#
5th

B
♭7th

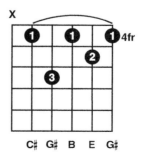

4fr

C# G# B E G#

C♯add9

C-sharp added ninth

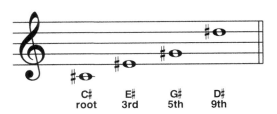

C♯	E♯	G♯	D♯
root	3rd	5th	9th

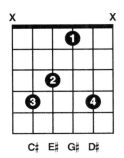

X   X

C♯ E♯ G♯ D♯

C♯sus2 (C♯5add2)

C-sharp suspended second

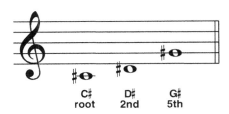

C♯	D♯	G♯
root	2nd	5th

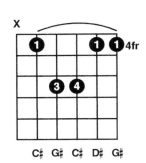

X

4fr

C♯ G♯ C♯ D♯ G♯

C♯sus4 (C♯sus)

C-sharp suspended fourth

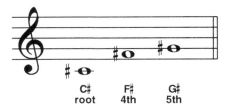

C♯	F♯	G♯
root	4th	5th

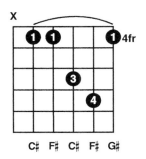

X

4fr

C♯ F♯ C♯ F♯ G♯

C♯7sus4 (C♯7sus)

C-sharp dominant seventh, suspended fourth

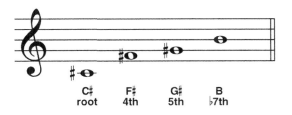

C♯	F♯	G♯	B
root	4th	5th	♭7th

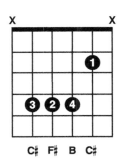

X   X

C♯ F♯ B C♯

C♯5 (C♯ no 3rd)
C-sharp fifth (power chord)

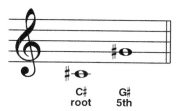

C♯
root

G♯
5th

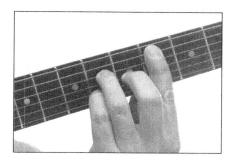

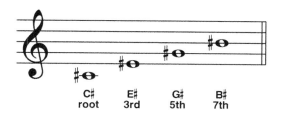

C♯ G♯ C♯

C♯+ (C♯aug, C♯(♯5))
C-sharp augmented

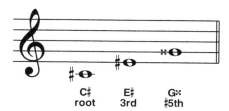

C♯
root

E♯
3rd

G𝄪
♯5th

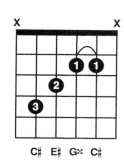

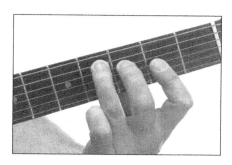

C♯ E♯ G𝄪 C♯

C♯maj7 (C♯M7)
C-sharp major seventh

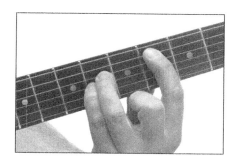

C♯
root

E♯
3rd

G♯
5th

B♯
7th

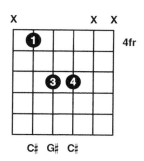

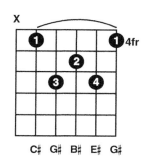

C♯ G♯ B♯ E♯ G♯

C♯°7 (C♯dim7)
C-sharp diminished seventh

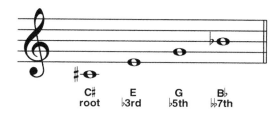

C♯
root

E
♭3rd

G
♭5th

B♭
♭♭7th

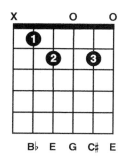

B♭ E G C♯ E

D (Dmaj)
D major

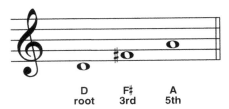

D	F#	A
root	3rd	5th

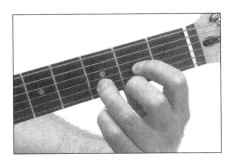 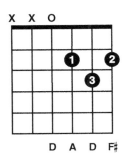

D A D F#

Dm (Dmin, D-)
D minor

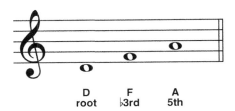

D	F	A
root	b3rd	5th

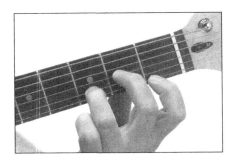 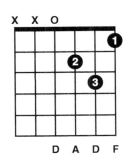

D A D F

D7 (Ddom7)
D dominant seventh

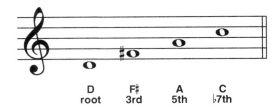

D	F#	A	C
root	3rd	5th	b7th

 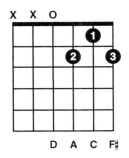

D A C F#

Dm7 (D-7, Dmin7)
D minor seventh

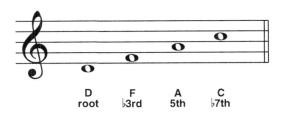

D	F	A	C
root	b3rd	5th	b7th

 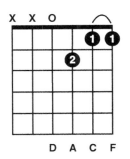

D A C F

Dadd9
D added ninth

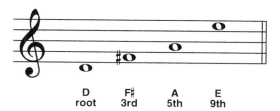

D	F#	A	E
root	3rd	5th	9th

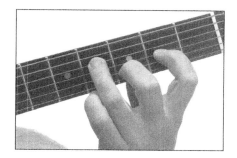 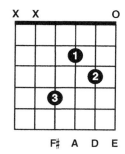

F# A D E

Dsus2 (D5add2)
D suspended second

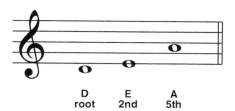

D	E	A
root	2nd	5th

 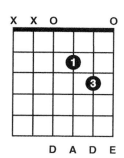

D A D E

Dsus4 (Dsus)
D suspended fourth

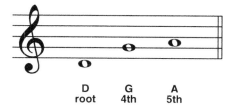

D	G	A
root	4th	5th

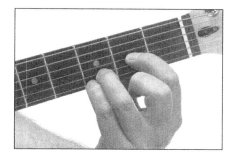 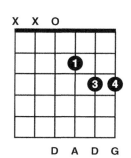

D A D G

D7sus4 (D7sus)
D dominant seventh, suspended fourth

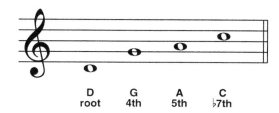

D	G	A	C
root	4th	5th	♭7th

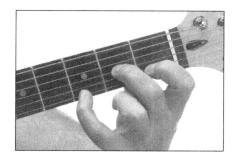 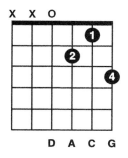

D A C G

D5 (D no 3rd)
D fifth (power chord)

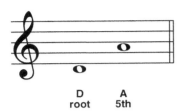

     D   A
   root   5th

X X O   X

D A D

D+ (Daug, D(♯5))
D augmented

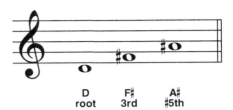

   D   F♯   A♯
 root   3rd ♯5th

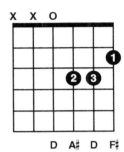

X X O

D A♯ D F♯

Dmaj7 (DM7)
D major seventh

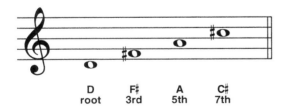

   D   F♯   A   C♯
 root 3rd 5th 7th

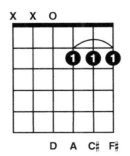

X X O

D A C♯ F♯

D°7 (Ddim7)
D diminished seventh

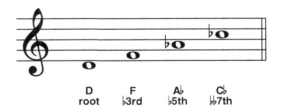

   D   F   A♭   C♭
 root ♭3rd ♭5th ♭♭7th

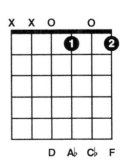

X X O   O

D A♭ C♭ F

E♭ (E♭maj)
E-flat major

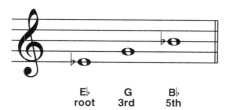

E♭	G	B♭
root	3rd	5th

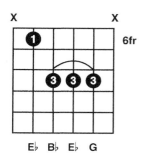

X · · · X · · 6fr
① · · ·
③ ③ ③

E♭ B♭ E♭ G

E♭m (E♭min, E♭-)
E-flat minor

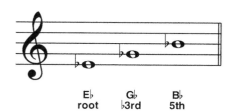

E♭	G♭	B♭
root	♭3rd	5th

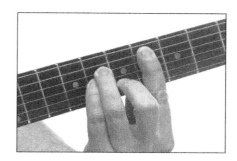

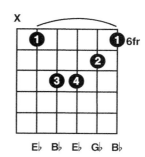

X
① · · ① 6fr
· · ② ·
③ ④ ·

E♭ B♭ E♭ G♭ B♭

E♭7 (E♭dom7)
E-flat dominant seventh

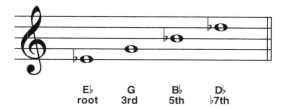

E♭	G	B♭	D♭
root	3rd	5th	♭7th

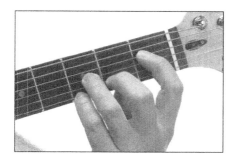

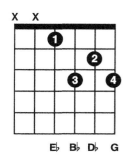

X X
① ·
· ②
③ · ④

E♭ B♭ D♭ G

E♭m7 (E♭min7, E♭-7)
E-flat minor seventh

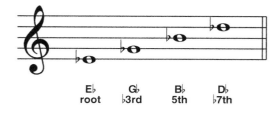

E♭	G♭	B♭	D♭
root	♭3rd	5th	♭7th

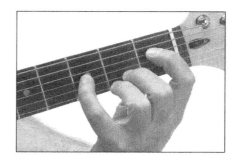

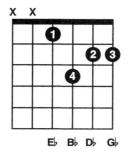

X X
① ·
· ② ③
④ ·

E♭ B♭ D♭ G♭

E♭add9
E-flat added ninth

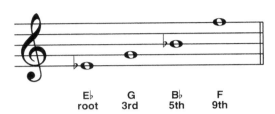

E♭	G	B♭	F
root	3rd	5th	9th

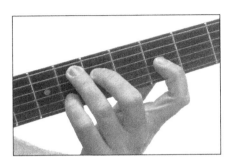
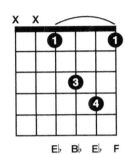

X   X

3fr

E♭   G   B♭   F

E♭sus2   (E♭5add2)
E-flat suspended second

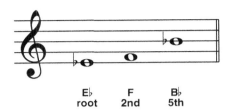

E♭	F	B♭
root	2nd	5th

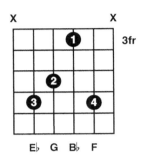

X   X

E♭   B♭   E♭   F

E♭sus4   (E♭sus)
E-flat suspended fourth

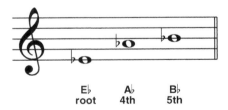

E♭	A♭	B♭
root	4th	5th

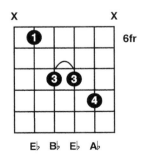

X   X

6fr

E♭   B♭   E♭   A♭

E♭7sus4   (E♭7sus)
E-flat dominant seventh, suspended fourth

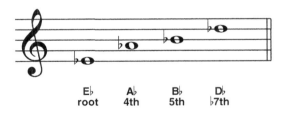

E♭	A♭	B♭	D♭
root	4th	5th	♭7th

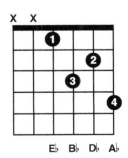

X   X

E♭   B♭   D♭   A♭

E♭5 (E♭ no 3rd)
E-flat fifth (power chord)

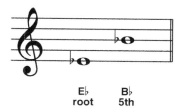

E♭ B♭
root 5th

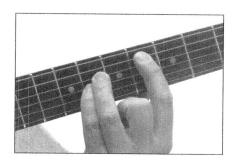

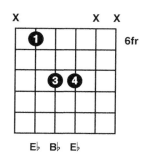

X   X X
6fr

E♭ B♭ E♭

E♭+ (E♭aug, E♭(♯5))
E-flat augmented

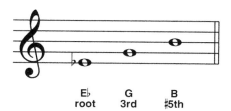

E♭ G B
root 3rd ♯5th

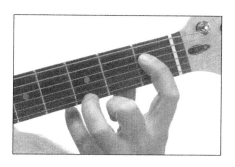

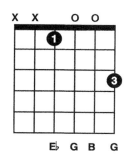

X X O O

E♭ G B G

E♭maj7 (E♭M7)
E-flat major seventh

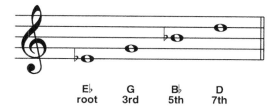

E♭ G B♭ D
root 3rd 5th 7th

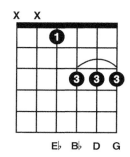

X X

E♭ B♭ D G

E♭°7 (E♭dim7)
E-flat diminished seventh

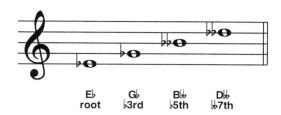

E♭ G♭ B♭♭ D♭♭
root ♭3rd ♭5th ♭♭7th

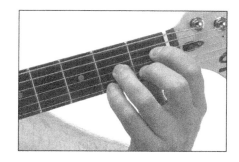

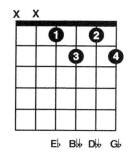

X X

E♭ B♭♭ D♭♭ G♭

E (Emaj)
E major

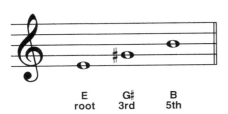

E root | G# 3rd | B 5th

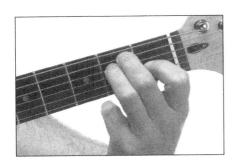 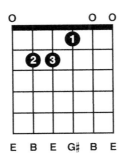

E B E G# B E

Em (Emin, E-)
E minor

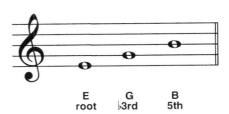

E root | G ♭3rd | B 5th

 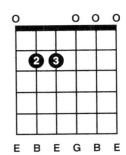

E B E G B E

E7 (Edom7)
E dominant seventh

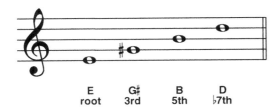

E root | G# 3rd | B 5th | D ♭7th

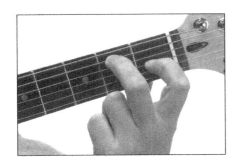 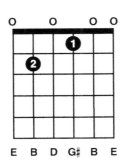

E B D G# B E

Em7 (Emin7, E-7)
E minor seventh

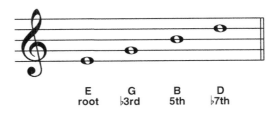

E root | G ♭3rd | B 5th | D ♭7th

 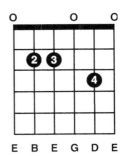

E B E G D E

Eadd9
E added ninth

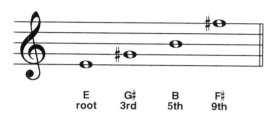

| E root | G♯ 3rd | B 5th | F♯ 9th |

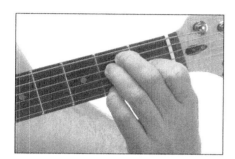

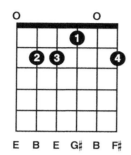

E B E G♯ B F♯

Esus2 (E5add2)
E suspended second

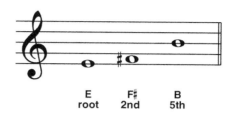

| E root | F♯ 2nd | B 5th |

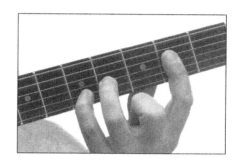

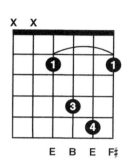

X X

E B E F♯

Esus4 (Esus)
E suspended fourth

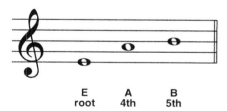

| E root | A 4th | B 5th |

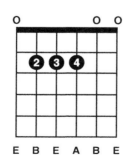

E B E A B E

E7sus4 (E7sus)
E dominant seventh, suspended fourth

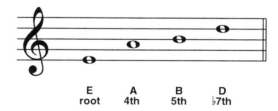

| E root | A 4th | B 5th | D ♭7th |

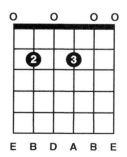

E B D A B E

E5 (E no 3rd)
E fifth (power chord)

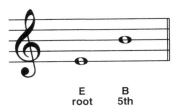

E   B
root   5th

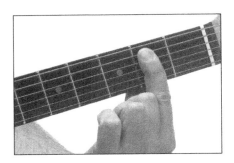 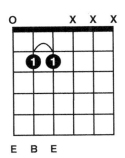

O   X X X

E B E

E+ (Eaug, E(♯5))
E augmented

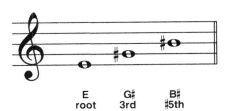

E   G♯   B♯
root   3rd   ♯5th

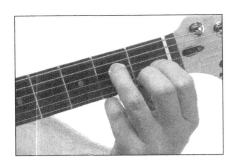 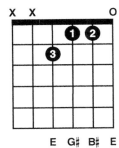

X X   O

E G♯ B♯ E

Emaj7 (EM7)
E major seventh

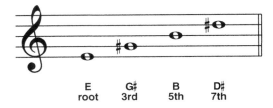

E   G♯   B   D♯
root   3rd   5th   7th

 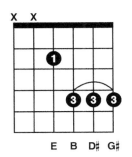

X X

E B D♯ G♯

E°7 (Edim7)
E diminished seventh

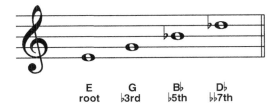

E   G   B♭   D♭
root ♭3rd ♭5th ♭♭7th

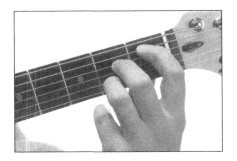 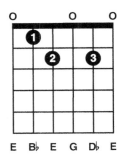

O   O   O

E B♭ E G D♭ E

F (Fmaj)
F major

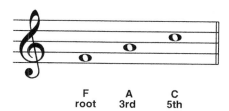

F A C
root 3rd 5th

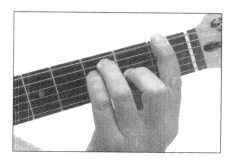 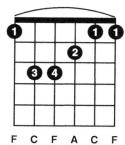

F C F A C F

F7 (Fdom7)
F dominant seventh

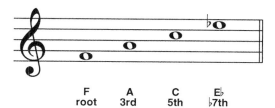

F A C E♭
root 3rd 5th ♭7th

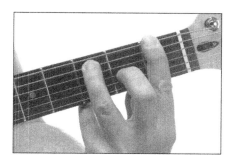 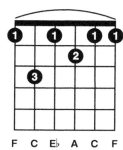

F C E♭ A C F

Fm (Fmin, F-)
F minor

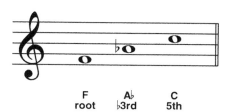

F A♭ C
root ♭3rd 5th

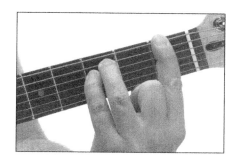 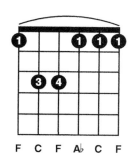

F C F A♭ C F

Fm7 (F-7, Fmin7)
F minor seventh

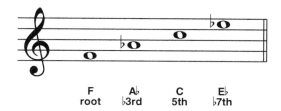

F A♭ C E♭
root ♭3rd 5th ♭7th

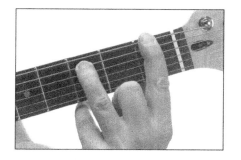 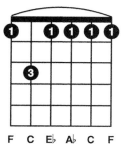

F C E♭ A♭ C F

Fadd9
F added ninth

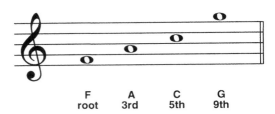

F A C G
root 3rd 5th 9th

X X

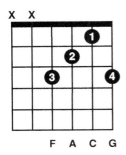

F A C G

Fsus2 (F5add2)
F suspended second

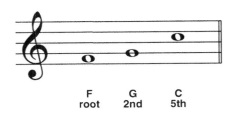

F G C
root 2nd 5th

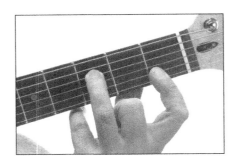

X X O

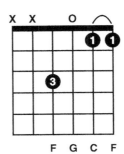

F G C F

Fsus4 (Fsus)
F suspended fourth

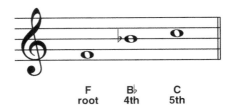

F B♭ C
root 4th 5th

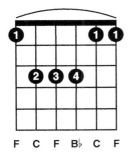

F C F B♭ C F

F7sus4 (F7sus)
F dominant seventh, suspended fourth

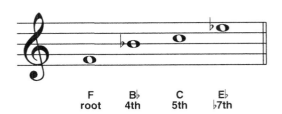

F B♭ C E♭
root 4th 5th ♭7th

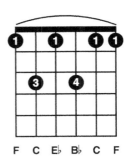

F C E♭ B♭ C F

F5 (F no 3rd)
F fifth (power chord)

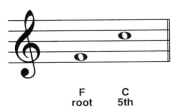

F	C
root	5th

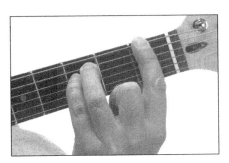

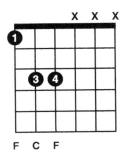

F C F

F+ (Faug, F(♯5))
F augmented

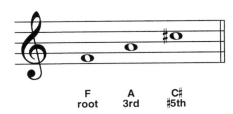

F	A	C♯
root	3rd	♯5th

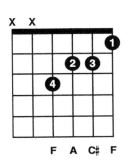

F A C♯ F

Fmaj7 (FM7)
F major seventh

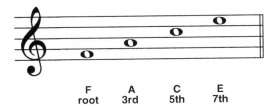

F	A	C	E
root	3rd	5th	7th

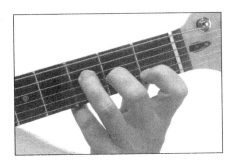

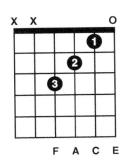

F A C E

F°7 (Fdim7)
F diminished seventh

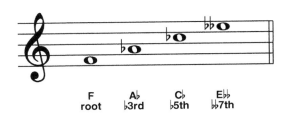

F	A♭	C♭	E♭♭
root	♭3rd	♭5th	♭♭7th

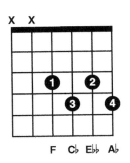

F C♭ E♭♭ A♭

F# (F#maj)
F-sharp major

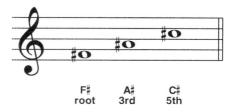

F#   A#   C#
root   3rd   5th

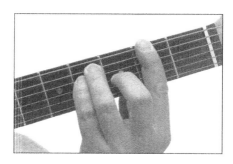 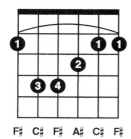

F# C# F# A# C# F#

F#m (F#-, F#min)
F-sharp minor

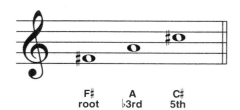

F#   A   C#
root   b3rd   5th

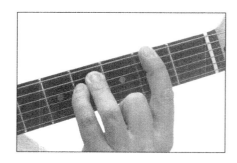 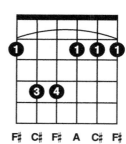

F# C# F# A C# F#

F#7 (F#dom7)
F-sharp dominant seventh

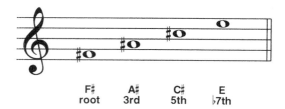

F#   A#   C#   E
root   3rd   5th   b7th

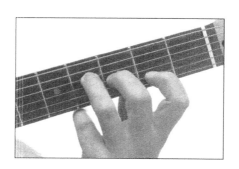 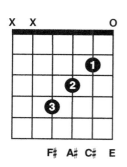

X   X   O

F# A# C# E

F#m7 (F#-7, F#min7)
F-sharp minor seventh

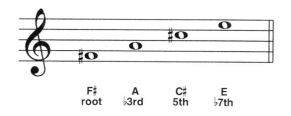

F#   A   C#   E
root   b3rd   5th   b7th

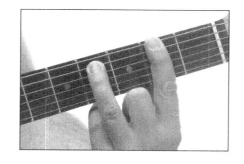 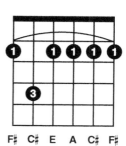

F# C# E A C# F#

F#add9
F-sharp added ninth

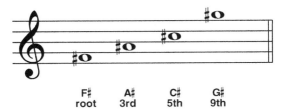

F#	A#	C#	G#
root	3rd	5th	9th

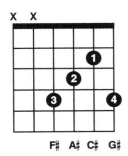

F#sus2 (F#5add2)
F-sharp suspended second

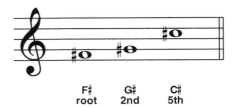

F#	G#	C#
root	2nd	5th

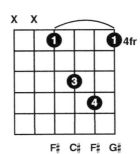

F#sus4 (F#sus)
F-sharp suspended fourth

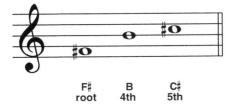

F#	B	C#
root	4th	5th

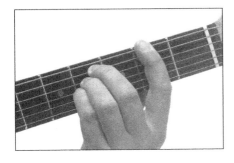

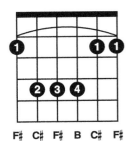

F#7sus4 (F#7sus)
F-sharp dominant seventh, suspended fourth

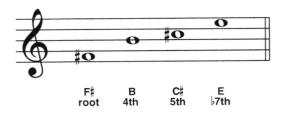

F#	B	C#	E
root	4th	5th	♭7th

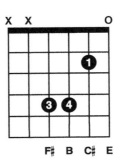

F#5 (F# no 3rd)
F-sharp fifth (power chord)

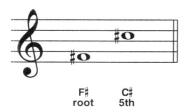

F#   C#
root   5th

X X X

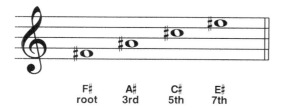

F#   C#   F#

F#+ (F#aug, F#(#5))
F-sharp augmented

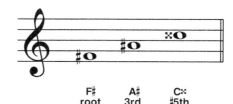

F#   A#   Cx
root   3rd   #5th

X X O

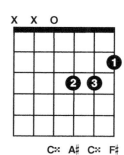

Cx   A#   Cx   F#

F#maj7 (F#M7)
F-sharp major seventh

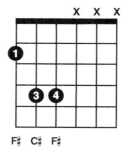

F#   A#   C#   E#
root   3rd   5th   7th

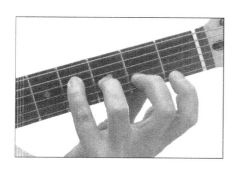

X X

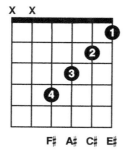

F#   A#   C#   E#

F#°7 (F#dim7)
F-sharp diminished seventh

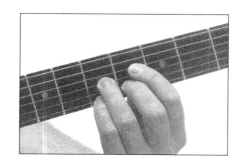

F#   A   C   Eb
root   b3rd   b5th   bb7th

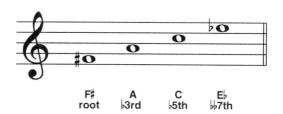

X X

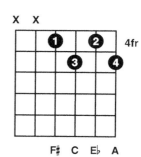

4fr

F#   C   Eb   A

G (Gmaj)
G major

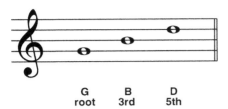

G
root

B
3rd

D
5th

 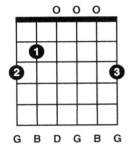

O O O

G B D G B G

Gm (G-, Gmin)
G minor

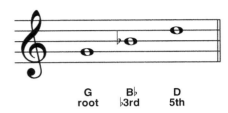

G
root

B♭
♭3rd

D
5th

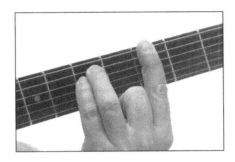 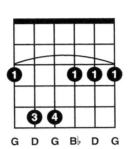

G D G B♭ D G

G7 (Gdom7)
G dominant seventh

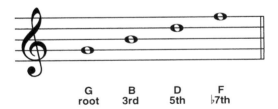

G
root

B
3rd

D
5th

F
♭7th

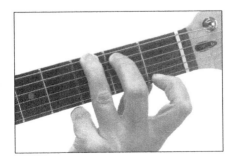 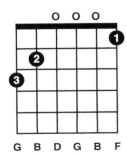

O O O

G B D G B F

Gm7 (G-7, Gmin7)
G minor seventh

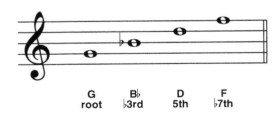

G
root

B♭
♭3rd

D
5th

F
♭7th

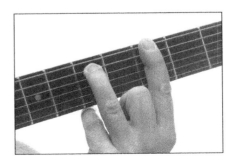 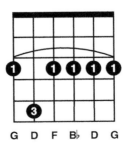

G D F B♭ D G

Gadd9
G added ninth

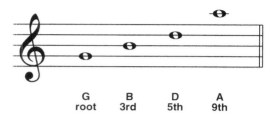

G	B	D	A
root	3rd	5th	9th

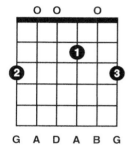

O   O   O

G A D A B G

Gsus2 (G5add2)
G suspended second

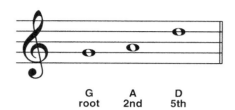

G	A	D
root	2nd	5th

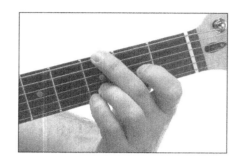
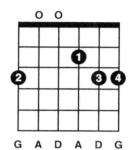

O   O

G A D A D G

Gsus4 (Gsus)
G suspended fourth

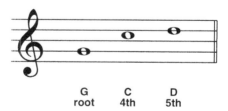

G	C	D
root	4th	5th

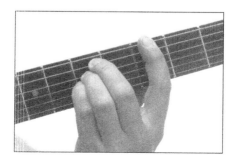
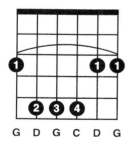

G D G C D G

G7sus4 (G7sus)
G dominant seventh, suspended fourth

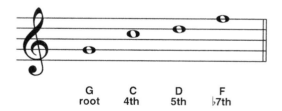

G	C	D	F
root	4th	5th	♭7th

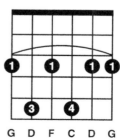

G D F C D G

G5 (G5 no 3rd)
G fifth (power chord)

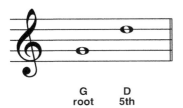

G D
root 5th

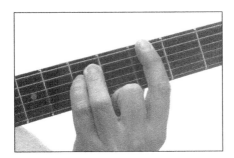

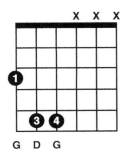

X X X

G D G

G+ (Gaug, G(♯5))
G augmented

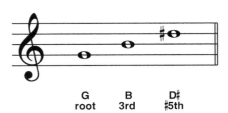

G B D♯
root 3rd ♯5th

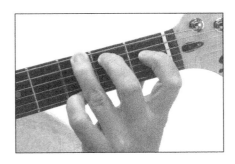

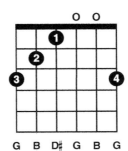

O O

G B D♯ G B G

Gmaj7 (GM7)
G major seventh

G B D F♯
root 3rd 5th 7th

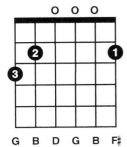

O O O

G B D G B F♯

G°7 (Gdim7)
G diminished seventh

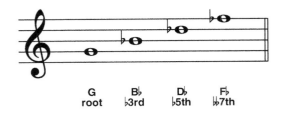

G B♭ D♭ F♭
root ♭3rd ♭5th ♭♭7th

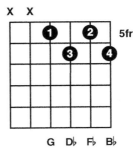

X X

5fr

G D♭ F♭ B♭

A♭ (A♭maj)
A-flat major

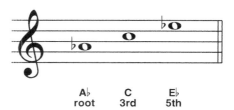

A♭   C   E♭
root   3rd   5th

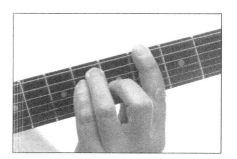 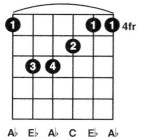

A♭ E♭ A♭ C E♭ A♭

A♭m (A♭min, A♭-)
A-flat minor

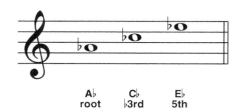

A♭   C♭   E♭
root   ♭3rd   5th

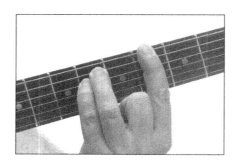 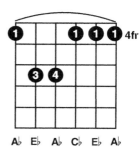

A♭ E♭ A♭ C♭ E♭ A♭

A♭7 (A♭dom7)
A-flat dominant seventh

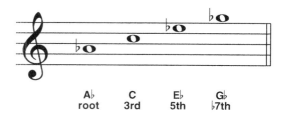

A♭   C   E♭   G♭
root   3rd   5th   ♭7th

 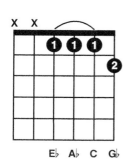

X X

E♭ A♭ C G♭

A♭m7 (A♭-7, A♭min7)
A-flat minor seventh

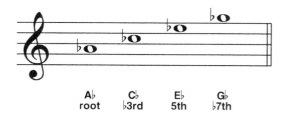

A♭   C♭   E♭   G♭
root   ♭3rd   5th   ♭7th

 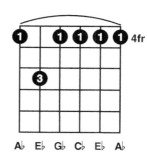

A♭ E♭ G♭ C♭ E♭ A♭

A♭add9
A-flat added ninth

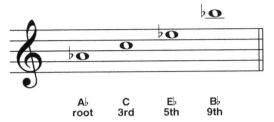

A♭	C	E♭	B♭
root	3rd	5th	9th

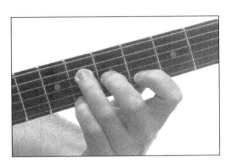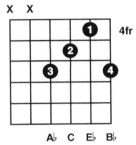

X X
4fr

A♭ C E♭ B♭

A♭sus2 (A♭5add2)
A-flat suspended second

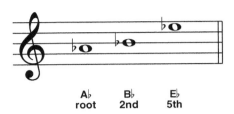

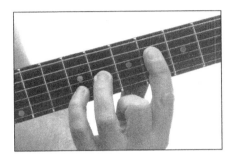

A♭	B♭	E♭
root	2nd	5th

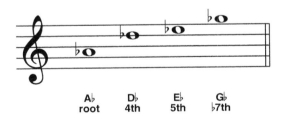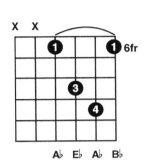

X X
6fr

A♭ E♭ A♭ B♭

A♭sus4 (A♭sus)
A-flat suspended fourth

A♭	D♭	E♭
root	4th	5th

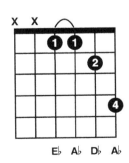

X X

E♭ A♭ D♭ A♭

A♭7sus4 (A♭7sus)
A-flat dominant seventh, suspended fourth

A♭	D♭	E♭	G♭
root	4th	5th	♭7th

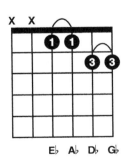

X X

E♭ A♭ D♭ G♭

A♭5 (A♭ no 3rd)
A-flat fifth (power chord)

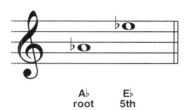

A♭   E♭
root   5th

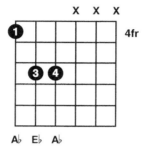

X   X   X

4fr

A♭   E♭   A♭

A♭+ (A♭aug, A♭(♯5))
A-flat augmented

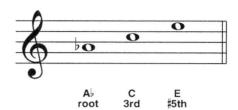

A♭   C   E
root   3rd   ♯5th

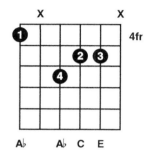

X   X

4fr

A♭   A♭   C   E

A♭maj7 (A♭M7)
A-flat major seventh

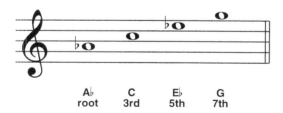

A♭   C   E♭   G
root   3rd   5th   7th

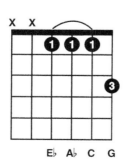

X   X

E♭   A♭   C   G

A♭°7 (A♭dim7)
A-flat diminished seventh

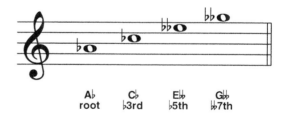

A♭   C♭   E♭♭   G♭♭
root   ♭3rd   ♭5th   ♭♭7th

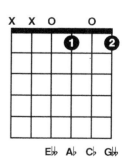

X   X   O   O

E♭♭   A♭   C♭   G♭♭

A (Amaj)
A major

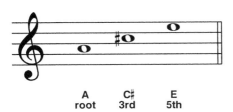

A · C♯ · E
root · 3rd · 5th

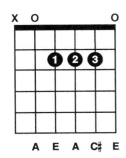

A E A C♯ E

Am (Amin, A-)
A minor

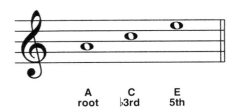

A · C · E
root · ♭3rd · 5th

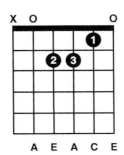

A E A C E

A7 (Adom7)
A dominant seventh

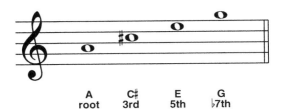

A · C♯ · E · G
root · 3rd · 5th · ♭7th

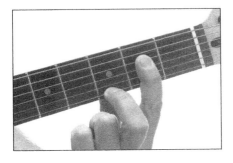

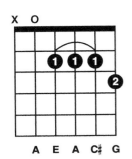

A E A C♯ G

Am7 (A-7, Amin7)
A minor seventh

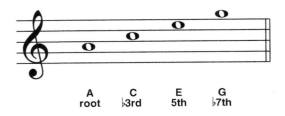

A · C · E · G
root · ♭3rd · 5th · ♭7th

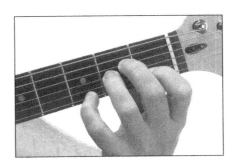

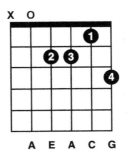

A E A C G

Aadd9
A added ninth

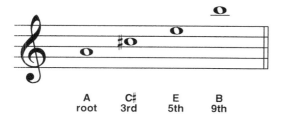

A	C#	E	B
root	3rd	5th	9th

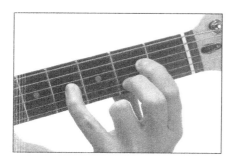
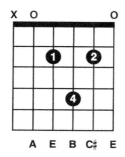

A E B C# E

Asus2 (A5add2)
A suspended second

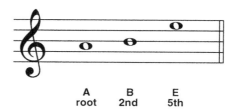

A	B	E
root	2nd	5th

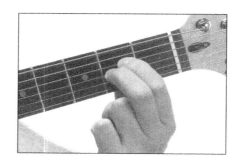
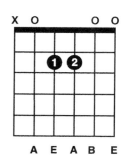

A E A B E

Asus4 (Asus)
A suspended fourth

A	D	E
root	4th	5th

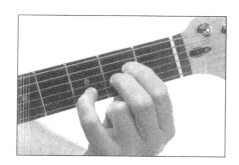
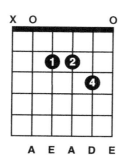

A E A D E

A7sus4 (A7sus)
A dominant seventh, suspended fourth

A	D	E	G
root	4th	5th	♭7th

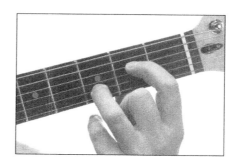
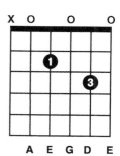

A E G D E

A5 (A no 3rd)
A fifth (power chord)

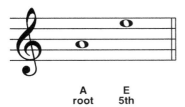

A   E
root   5th

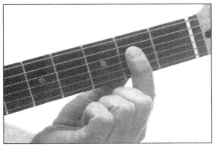

X O   X X

A E A

A+ (Aaug, A(♯5))
A augmented

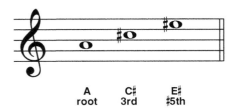

A   C♯   E♯
root   3rd ♯5th

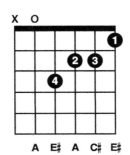

X O

A E♯ A C♯ E♯

Amaj7 (AM7)
A major seventh

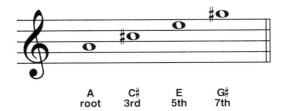

A   C♯   E   G♯
root   3rd   5th 7th

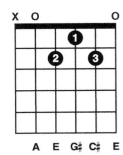

X O   O

A E G♯ C♯ E

A°7 (Adim7)
A diminished seventh

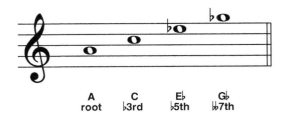

A   C   E♭   G♭
root ♭3rd ♭5th ♭♭7th

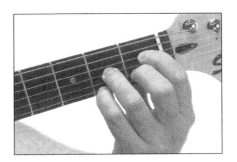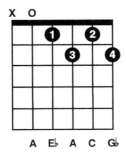

X O

A E♭ A C G♭

B♭ (B♭maj)
B-flat major

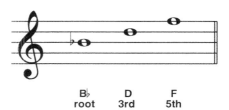

B♭   D   F
root   3rd   5th

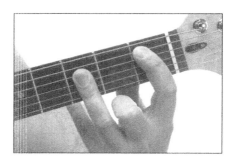
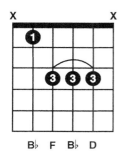

B♭   F   B♭   D

B♭m (B♭min, B♭-)
B-flat minor

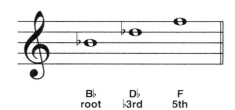

B♭   D♭   F
root   ♭3rd   5th

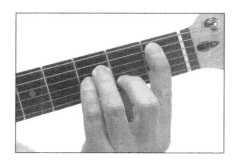
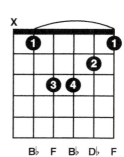

B♭   F   B♭   D♭   F

B♭7 (B♭dom7)
B-flat dominant seventh

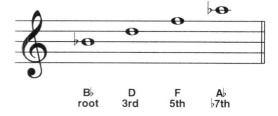

B♭   D   F   A♭
root   3rd   5th   ♭7th

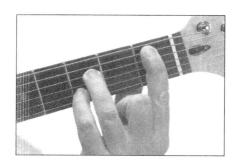
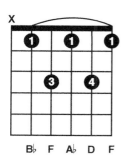

B♭   F   A♭   D   F

B♭m7 (B♭-7, B♭min7)
B-flat minor seventh

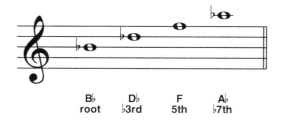

B♭   D♭   F   A♭
root   ♭3rd   5th   ♭7th

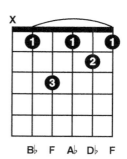

B♭   F   A♭   D♭   F

B♭add9
B-flat added ninth

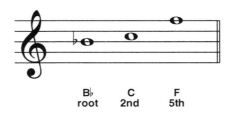

B♭	D	F	C
root	3rd	5th	9th

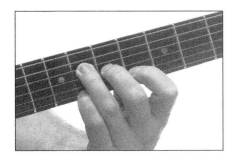

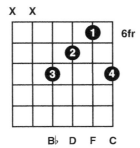

X X   6fr

B♭   D   F   C

B♭sus2   (B♭5add2)
B-flat suspended second

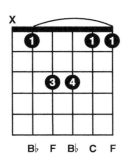

B♭	C	F
root	2nd	5th

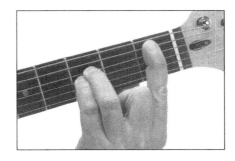

X

B♭   F   B♭   C   F

B♭sus4   (B♭sus)
B-flat suspended fourth

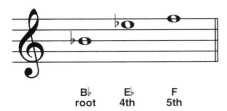

B♭	E♭	F
root	4th	5th

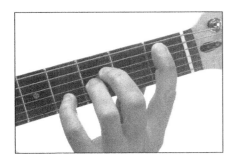

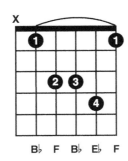

X

B♭   F   B♭   E♭   F

B♭7sus4   (B♭7sus)
B-flat dominant seventh, suspended fourth

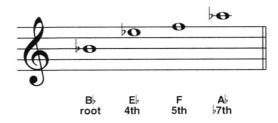

B♭	E♭	F	A♭
root	4th	5th	♭7th

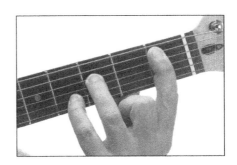

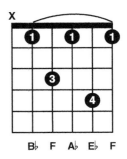

X

B♭   F   A♭   E♭   F

B♭5 (B♭ no 3rd)
B-flat fifth (power chord)

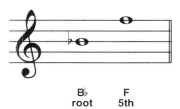

B♭	F
root	5th

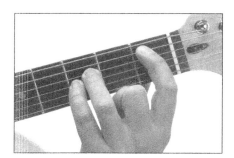
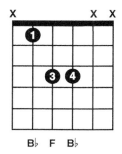

B♭ F B♭

B♭+ (B♭aug, B♭(♯5))
B-flat augmented

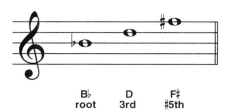

B♭	D	F♯
root	3rd	♯5th

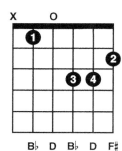

B♭ D B♭ D F♯

B♭maj7 (B♭M7)
B-flat major seventh

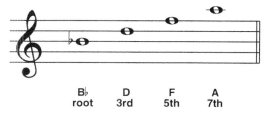

B♭	D	F	A
root	3rd	5th	7th

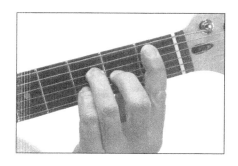
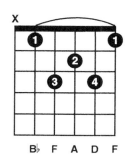

B♭ F A D F

B♭°7 (B♭dim7)
B-flat diminished seventh

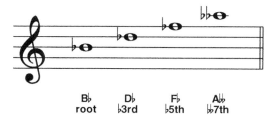

B♭	D♭	F♭	A♭♭
root	♭3rd	♭5th	♭♭7th

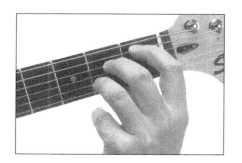
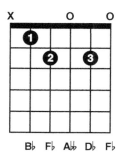

B♭ F♭ A♭♭ D♭ F♭

B (Bmaj)
B major

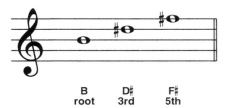

B — root
D# — 3rd
F# — 5th

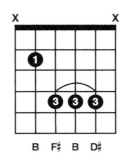

X | | | | X

① ... ③ ③ ③

B F# B D#

Bm (Bmin, B-)
B minor

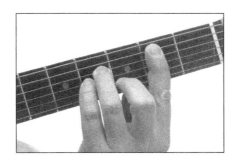

B — root
D — b3rd
F# — 5th

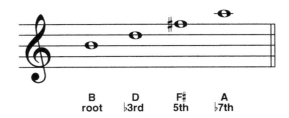
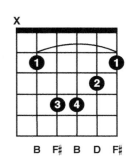

X

① ... ①
②
③ ④

B F# B D F#

B7 (Bdom7)
B dominant seventh

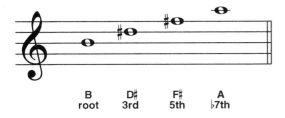

B — root
D# — 3rd
F# — 5th
A — b7th

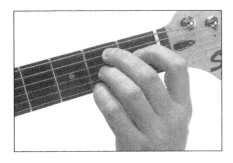
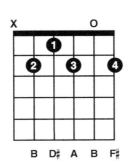

X | | | | O

①
② ③ ④

B D# A B F#

Bm7 (B-7, Bmin7)
B minor seventh

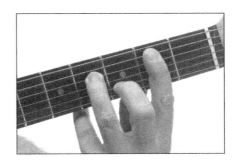

B — root
D — b3rd
F# — 5th
A — b7th

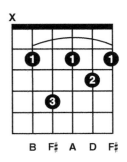

X

① ① ①
②
③

B F# A D F#

Badd9
B added ninth

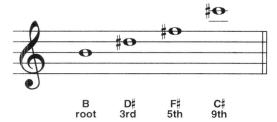

B	D#	F#	C#
root	3rd	5th	9th

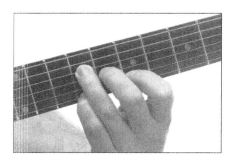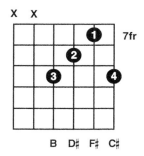

B D# F# C#

Bsus2 (B5add2)
B suspended second

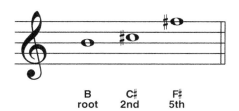

B	C#	F#
root	2nd	5th

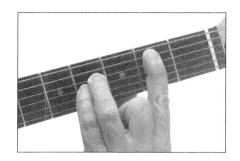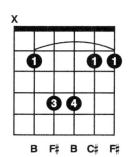

B F# B C# F#

Bsus4 (Bsus)
B suspended fourth

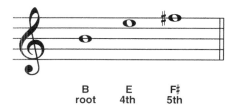

B	E	F#
root	4th	5th

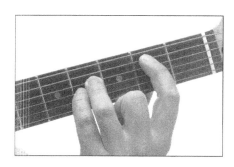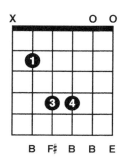

B F# B B E

B7sus4 (B7sus)
B dominant seventh, suspended fourth

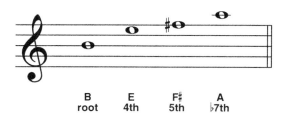

B	E	F#	A
root	4th	5th	b7th

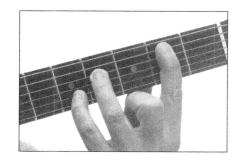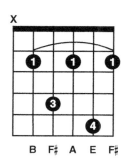

B F# A E F#

B5 (B no 3rd)
B fifth (power chord)

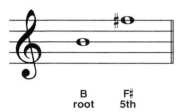

B — root
F# — 5th

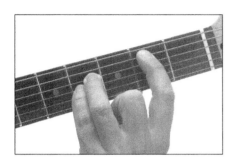 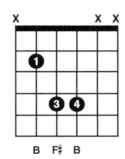

B F# B

B+ (Baug, B(♯5))
B augmented

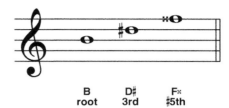

B — root
D# — 3rd
F𝄪 — ♯5th

 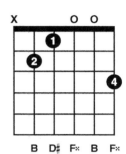

B D# F𝄪 B F𝄪

Bmaj7 (BM7)
B major seventh

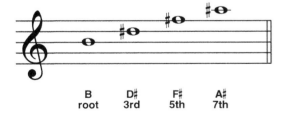

B — root
D# — 3rd
F# — 5th
A# — 7th

 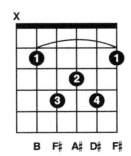

B F# A# D# F#

B°7 (Bdim7)
B diminished seventh

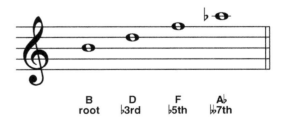

B — root
D — ♭3rd
F — ♭5th
A♭ — ♭♭7th

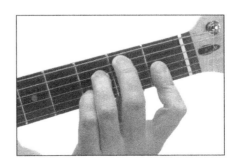 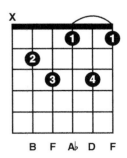

B F A♭ D F

CHRISTIAN SONGBOOKS
FOR EASY GUITAR

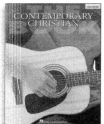

THE CONTEMPORARY CHRISTIAN BOOK
A huge collection of 85 CCM favorites arranged for beginning-level guitarists. Includes: Abba (Father) • Above All • Awesome God • Beautiful • Dive • Friends • His Eyes • How Great Is Our God • Jesus Freak • Lifesong • Mountain of God • This Is Your Time • Wholly Yours • Word of God Speak • and more.
00702195 Easy Guitar (No Tab)......................$17.99

THE CONTEMPORARY CHRISTIAN COLLECTION
INCLUDES TAB Easy arrangements of 50 Christian hits, complete with tab! Includes: Alive Again • All Because of Jesus • Beautiful • Big House • By Your Side • Dive • Enough • Give Me Your Eyes • Hold My Heart • Joy • Live Out Loud • More • Song of Hope • Undo • Wholly Yours • The Word Is Alive • and dozens more!
00702283 Easy Guitar with Notes & Tab.........$16.99

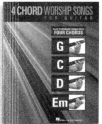

4-CHORD WORSHIP SONGS FOR GUITAR
PLAY 25 WORSHIP SONGS WITH FOUR CHORDS: G-C-D-Em
More than two dozen Christian hits that guitarists can play using just four chords! Includes: All We Need • Ancient Words • Awesome God • Breathe • Everyday • Forever • I Will Rise • Love the Lord • No One like You • Unchanging • more!
00701727 Guitar Chords....................................$10.99

GUITAR WORSHIP METHOD SONGBOOK BOOK 1
Book/CD Pack
This book can be used on its own, as a supplement to *Guitar Worship Method Book 1* (00695681) or with any other guitar method. You get lyrics, chord frames, strumming patterns, and a full-band CD, so you can hear how each song sounds and then play along when you're ready. Songs include: Better Is One Day • Blessed Be Your Name • Breathe • Forever • Here I Am to Worship • I Could Sing of Your Love Forever • Lord, Reign in Me • You Are My King (Amazing Love).
00699641 Lyrics/Chord Frames $14.99

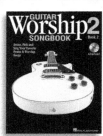

GUITAR WORSHIP METHOD SONGBOOK 2
INCLUDES TAB *Book/CD Pack*
12 more songs with lyrics, chord frames, strumming patterns and a full-band CD that you can use for your worship-playing needs. Songs include: Awesome God • Enough • Give Us Clean Hands • God of Wonders • The Heart of Worship • How Great Is Our God • In Christ Alone • Mighty to Save • Shout to the Lord • Sing to the King • Step by Step • We Fall Down.
00701082 Guitar Arrangements $14.99

PRAISE AND WORSHIP FOR GUITAR
INCLUDES TAB Easy arrangements of 45 beautiful Praise and Worship songs, including: As the Deer • Be Not Afraid • Emmanuel • Glorify Thy Name • Great Is the Lord • He Is Exalted • Holy Ground • Lamb of God • Majesty • Thou Art Worthy • We Bow Down • You Are My Hiding Place • and more.
00702125 Easy Guitar with Notes & Tab.........$10.99

3-CHORD WORSHIP SONGS FOR GUITAR
PLAY 24 WORSHIP SONGS WITH THREE CHORDS: G-C-D
Two dozen tunes playable on guitar using only G, C and D chords. Includes: Agnus Dei • Because We Believe • Enough • Father I Adore You • Here I Am to Worship • Step by Step • There Is a Redeemer • We Fall Down • Worthy, You Are Worthy • and more. No tab.
00701131 Guitar Chords....................................$10.99

TOP WORSHIP HITS
INCLUDES TAB Easier arrangements perfect for guitarists who want to join in the worship service. Includes 30 songs: Beautiful One • Blessed Be Your Name • God of Wonders • Hosanna (Praise Is Rising) • I Give You My Heart • Mighty to Save • Revelation Song • Sing to the King • Your Grace Is Enough • and more.
00702294 Easy Guitar with Notes & Tab.........$15.99

THE WORSHIP BOOK
Easy arrangements (no tab) of 80 great worship tunes, including: Above All • Days of Elijah • Forever • Here I Am to Worship • Mighty to Save • Open the Eyes of My Heart • Shout to the Lord • Sing to the King • We Fall Down • and more.
00702247 Easy Guitar (No Tab)......................$15.99

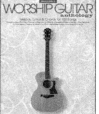

THE WORSHIP GUITAR ANTHOLOGY – VOLUME 1
This collection contains melody, lyrics & chords for 100 contemporary favorites, such as: Beautiful One • Forever • Here I Am to Worship • Hosanna (Praise Is Rising) • How He Loves • In Christ Alone • Mighty to Save • Our God • Revelation Song • Your Grace Is Enough • and dozens more.
00101864 Melody/Lyrics/Chords.....................$16.99

CHORDBUDDY GUITAR LEARNING SYSTEM – WORSHIP EDITION
ChordBuddy Media
As soon as the ChordBuddy is properly attached to your acoustic or electric guitar, you will be able to make music instantly. Within a few weeks, you'll begin removing some of the tabs and making the chords on your own. In two months, you'll be able to play the guitar with no ChordBuddy at all! Package Includes: ChordBuddy • instruction book • companion DVD with a 2-month lesson plan • and ChordBuddy songbook with 60 songs. This Worship Edition uses songs in both the songbook and instructional book that are geared for Sunday school, praise and worship bands, and more.
00124638 Songbook with ChordBuddy Device & DVD..........................$49.95

CHORDBUDDY WORSHIP SONGBOOK
ChordBuddy Media
This songbook includes 60 timeless Christian tunes in color-coded arrangements that correspond to the device colors: Awesome God • Because of Your Love • Create in Me a Clean Heart • I Could Sing of Your Love Forever • Jesus Loves Me • Kum Ba Yah • More Precious Than Silver • Rock of Ages • Shout to the North • This Little Light of Mine • and more. ChordBuddy device is sold separately.
00127895 Book Only $14.99

HAL•LEONARD®
www.halleonard.com

Prices, contents and availability subject to change without notice.

0917